FUN WITH CHEMISTRY

by

MAE and IRA FREEMAN

RANDOM HOUSE • NEW YORK

CONTENTS

When Charles Goodyear dropped a piece of rubber mixed with sulphur on a hot stove, he accidentally discovered the process by which rubber could be vulcanized

WHAT CHEMISTRY IS ABOUT

When you look around you at home, at school, or outdoors you see a great many different materials—a wooden table, a glass window, a brass doorknob, a piece of chalk, a pool of water, or a cement sidewalk.

The business of the chemist is to study different kinds of matter such as these and hundreds of thousands of others. He not only learns what things are made of, but also finds out how to make new materials by putting familiar ones together in new and different ways. You probably know already about some of the new foods and drugs he has manufactured in order to keep us healthy. We see an amazing fabric that is made from coal, water and air; our lives are made brighter, safer and more comfortable by gleaming plastics and shiny new metals.

Until only three hundred years ago chemistry as we know it today did not exist. Instead of trying to understand the materials around them, experimenters worked at the hopeless task of trying to make gold out of iron. Gradually, more scientific ways of looking at things were developed, but the large scale production of new chemical products began only about thirty years ago.

In this book you will find out how chemists work some of their modern miracles, and the way you will learn is by trying simple, interesting experiments that can be done right at home. The materials required for your laboratory work are to be found in the kitchen or in the medicine cabinet. All you will wish to buy are three or four test tubes which cost only a few pennies at the drug store. None of the experiments is dangerous or messy.

5

HOW TO MAKE A TEST TUBE HOLDER

A useful piece of equipment you can make to help carry on some of your chemical experiments is a test tube holder. This is needed to hold the tube while it is being heated over a flame. The pictures on the opposite page show how to go about making one.

Get an ordinary coat hanger made of thin wire and untwist the ends where they are joined. Straighten out a piece about a foot long and cut it off by holding it with a pair of pliers and bending it back and forth several times.

Now find a piece of pipe or a round stick of wood which is about the same size as the test tubes you have. Hold one end of the wire firmly against the pipe or stick with the pliers, and bend two or three coils of wire around in a spiral (see second picture). Remove the pipe and bend the other end of the wire into a loop to form a handle. Try the tube in the holder and adjust the coils to see that the tube goes in easily, yet stops when the turned-back lip rests on the first coil.

In heating a material in a test tube, do not heat the very bottom of the tube but hold it at a slant, with the flame under the side of the tube just _above_ the bottom, as in the photograph. And, of course, always point the open end of the tube off to one side—never toward your face—in case the contents should spatter. A chemist who burns himself is a poor worker and should be fully as ashamed of himself as a carpenter who is careless enough to hit his thumb with a hammer!

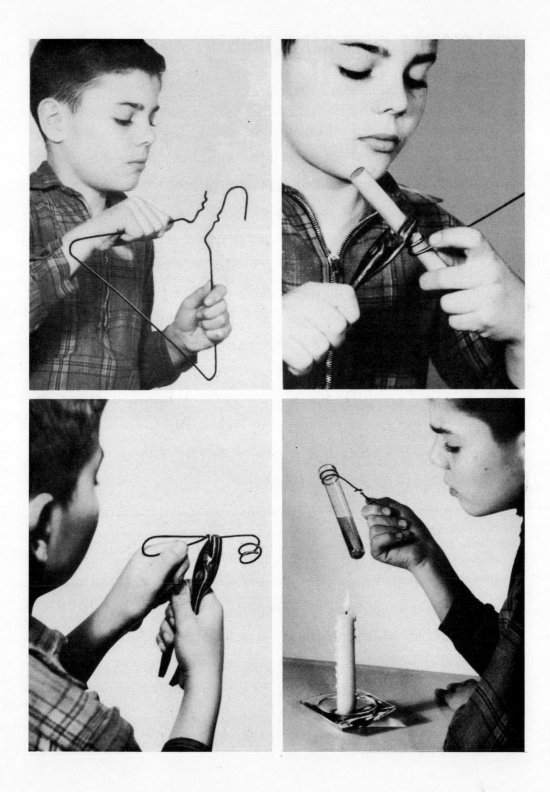

MAKING OTHER CHEMICAL EQUIPMENT

Another simple piece of apparatus you will need is the test tube rack shown in the upper left hand picture opposite. Make it by removing one side of a cardboard box and cutting three or four holes in the top, each hole being just big enough to hold a test tube.

One of the best ways to pour a powder into a vessel is first to dump the powder onto a piece of stiff paper that has been creased down the middle to form a trough, as shown in the upper right hand picture.

In the photograph, the powder is being poured into a measuring glass—another useful object for your home laboratory. It is made by sticking a strip of adhesive tape along the side of a small glass—one that holds about a cupful of liquid. Divide the length of the strip into four equal parts and mark them as shown. Then, for example, to measure out three-quarters of a cup of liquid, fill the glass until the liquid surface stands at the "¾" mark.

For pouring liquids into a narrow-necked bottle, make a funnel as shown in the three lower pictures. Cut a six-inch square of paper—wax paper is best but heavy wrapping paper will do. Fold in half each way as indicated. Snip off the very tip of the folded corner. Open out the paper to form a cone, so that there are three thicknesses of paper on one side and one thickness on the other. The funnel is then ready to use.

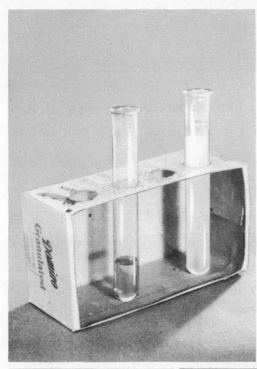

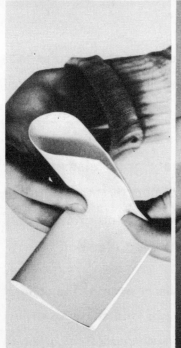
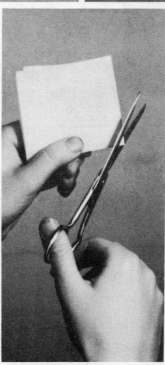

ATOMS AND MOLECULES

Scientists have found that every kind of material consists of very small particles called molecules, each far smaller than anything you can see even with the most powerful microscope. A hundred million molecules side by side would make a row only an inch long! Between the molecules there are spaces. This means that everything we think of as "solid" is really "full of holes"—the empty places between the molecules.

Try an experiment in order to get an idea of the fact that there are spaces in what seems to be solid matter. Fill a small glass with cotton. Fill another glass with water. If you are careful, you can then pour the full glass of water into the full glass of cotton and make them occupy the same space, as the upper picture shows.

Each variety of matter, such as water, is made up of molecules that are all alike. These molecules are the smallest units of the chemical _compound_ we call water.

The molecules of a compound are, in turn, made up of _atoms_ of certain chemical _elements_. There are only ninety or so elements. But just as all the words of the language can be formed by combining the twenty-six letters of our alphabet in different ways, so the great variety of compounds can be made from less than a hundred elements.

The lower picture shows a model of a molecule of aspirin. The colored wooden balls represent the different kinds of atoms and show how they are connected in the compound. Chemists make such models in order to study how new materials may be created in the laboratory.

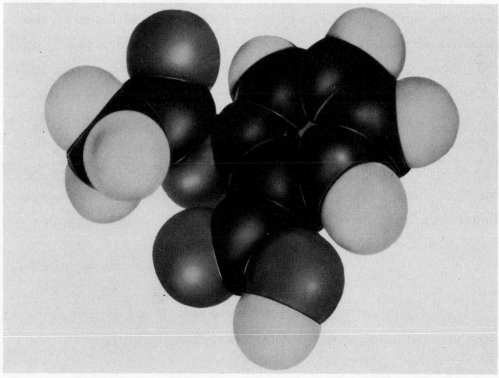

CRYSTALS OF SUGAR

When sugar is put into water it gradually dissolves until nothing appears to be left of it. What happens? The sugar separates into single molecules and they spread about in the spaces between the molecules of water. Because single molecules cannot be seen, the solution looks just as clear as plain water. But the sugar is still there, unchanged chemically, and you can get it back again.

Put three-quarters of a glassful of water into a pan and bring it to a boil. Turn the flame low and stir granulated cane sugar into the water, little by little, until no more will dissolve. This may take two to three cupfuls. Pour the mixture into a glass. Across the top of the glass lay a pencil that has a short length of cotton string tied to it. The string should reach almost to the bottom. A small weight such as a carpet tack or paper clip may be used to make the string hang straight down into the liquid.

Set the glass away in a warm place for several days and soon you will see that the string is covered with many-sided *crystals* of sugar. The solution, as it cooled, was no longer able to keep all of its sugar and had to give some of it up in the form of crystals. These crystals are of the same shape as the granulated sugar crystals you started with, but are larger. This "rock candy" can be eaten, but be sure that everything you have used in making it is clean.

Small crystals of sugar sometimes form in a jar of jam or honey that has been allowed to stand for a long time.

12

MORE ABOUT CRYSTALS

In the last experiment we saw that the crystals of rock candy and those of the sugar from which it was made had the same shape. This is a good example of the fact that a material can often be recognized by the form of its crystals. For instance, common salt has crystals that look like little cubes. Water, when it freezes, always forms six-sided crystals, and snowflakes always have this shape.

Many minerals and gems have special crystal shapes by which they can be recognized. These crystals formed ages ago when the melted materials in the hot interior of the earth began to cool. A diamond is merely a piece of crystallized carbon!

Let us try an experiment to show the shape of crystals of Epsom salts, or magnesium sulfate as the chemists call it. Put one-fourth of a glass of water into a small pan and heat it on the gas range. Add Epsom salts, stirring it in until no more will dissolve. This may take three or four teaspoonfuls. Remove from the stove and stir in one or two drops of ordinary liquid glue. When the glue has dissolved, swab some of the mixture evenly onto a piece of glass with a wad of cotton and set the glass aside.

In a few minutes, needle-like crystals will begin to appear in the liquid. You can actually watch them grow out in all directions, forming a pretty pattern. Soon the whole glass will seem to be covered with frost (see lower picture). When the water has dried completely you will have a sample of magnesium sulfate crystals that you can keep.

WATER FROM CRYSTALS

What seems to be a perfectly dry crystal may often have molecules of water locked up chemically inside of it. Ordinary washing soda, also called sal soda, is an example. The chemists' name for this compound is sodium carbonate.

Take a lump of washing soda and wipe it briskly with a cloth to rub off the white, powdery outer layer. Notice that the cleaned piece is clear and crystal-like. Break up this lump so that it can be put into a clean test tube. Heat the tube gently by holding it an inch or two above a candle flame. In a short time the pieces of soda will become wet and the steam that arises will have a crackling sound. The steam will condense in the cool upper part of the tube in the form of large drops (see picture). Soon only a dry, white powder will be left in the bottom of the tube.

Where did the water come from? The pieces you started with seemed perfectly dry. The fact is, however, that each molecule of sodium carbonate in a crystal has ten molecules of water hooked up with it chemically. When the crystals are heated, this water is driven off, as you have seen.

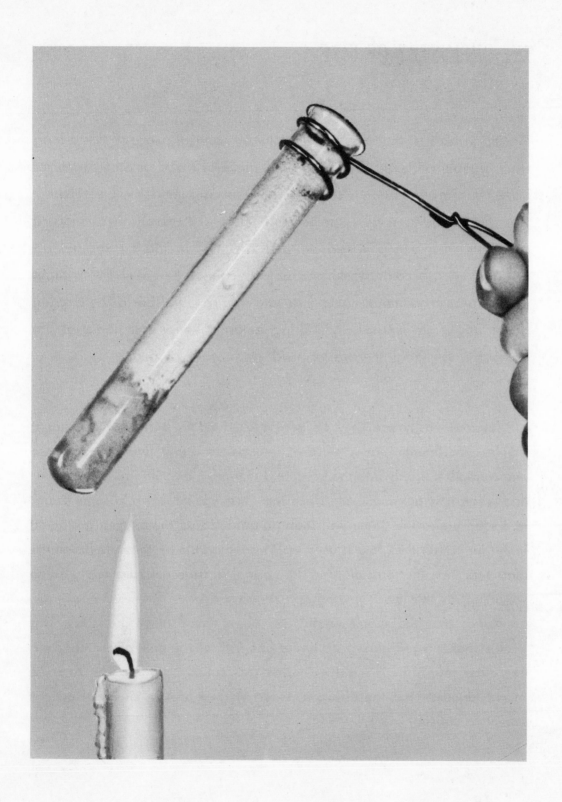

THE CHEMISTRY OF FIRE

Did you know that burning is really a chemical process? For a long while people believed that a burning piece of wood or other material gave up a mysterious, invisible fluid when consumed by fire. Then it was discovered that when something "burns" it merely means that it combines with a gas called oxygen which is in the air around us. Oxygen has no color, taste or odor. It cannot be seen. But without it, no breathing animal could live and no fire could burn. The oxygen taken into your lungs in breathing actually keeps the flame of life going by oxidizing the waste products in your blood.

You can easily see how oxygen is used up in burning by trying a simple experiment. Tear a piece of newspaper about five inches square and crumple it lightly into the bottom of a small glass. Set fire to the paper and when it is burning well, place the glass upside down in some water in a soup plate. The flame will soon go out because the oxygen contained in the air within the glass is used up. This makes the air pressure inside the glass less than that outside, and the normal outside pressure forces some water up, as the lower photograph shows.

Notice that the water finally fills about one-fifth of the glass. This means that oxygen makes up about one-fifth of the bulk of ordinary air. The other four-fifths is mainly another gas called *nitrogen*. The two are mixed together, but the nitrogen does not take part in chemical actions except in unusual cases.

18

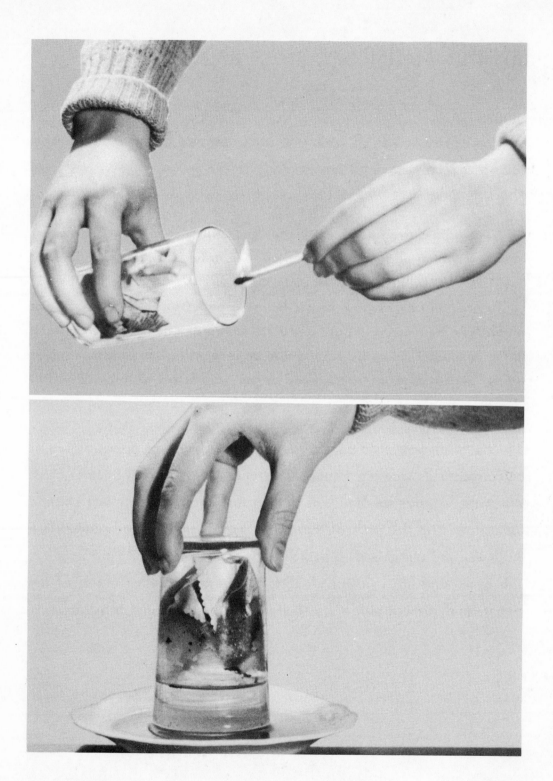

INVISIBLE WRITING

You can make use of what you have learned about oxidation by writing a secret message chemically.

Simply dip a clean pen into vinegar and write the message on a sheet of heavy writing paper. Dip the pen often in order to make a good heavy line. The "ink" will soon dry, leaving no trace.

To bring out the writing again, hold the paper an inch or two above a candle flame, moving it back and forth so that the heat is not too strong in any one place. Soon the writing will appear, traced in dark brown. For safety, work over a metal table-top or the drainboard of the sink.

The result you obtained depends on the fact that a material must be raised to its <u>kindling</u> <u>temperature</u> in order to make it burn or char. When the vinegar solution was put on the paper, a chemical change took place and this part of the paper was changed into a compound much like the ones used to make cellophane or film for your camera. This compound has a lower kindling temperature than the rest of the paper, and so heat made the written part oxidize and turn brown.

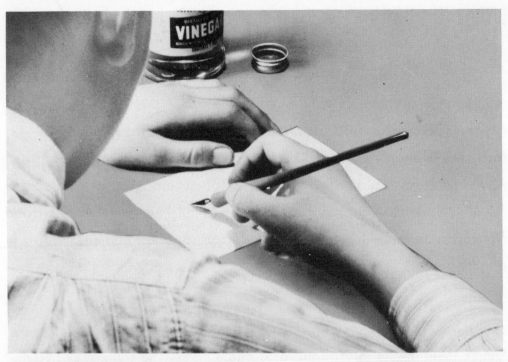

BURNING SUGAR

Sugar is a chemical compound made up of the elements carbon, oxygen and hydrogen. Carbon, as you know, is a black material—in fact, coal is mainly carbon. Oxygen and hydrogen are invisible gases. And yet this particular combination—sugar—is made up of white crystals that have a sweet taste, and is not at all like the elements from which it is formed. It is interesting to try to break down sugar by applying heat.

Wind a piece of thin wire around a lump of sugar. Using the wire as a handle, hold the lump of sugar in a candle flame. The sugar may become smudged from the flame or it may melt a little, but it will not actually burn. The black smudge is carbon from the candle flame and not from the sugar.

Now, touch a fresh corner of the sugar lump with a bit of cigarette ash. The smallest speck will be enough. Put this corner in the edge of the flame and in a second or so it will begin to burn with a pale blue flame, spouting out little smoke rings as in the lower photograph.

The shiny black mass that drips down as the sugar burns contains carbon that is set free when the compound breaks up. Have a dish handy to catch any drops that melt off, and be careful not to let any hot sugar drip onto your hand.

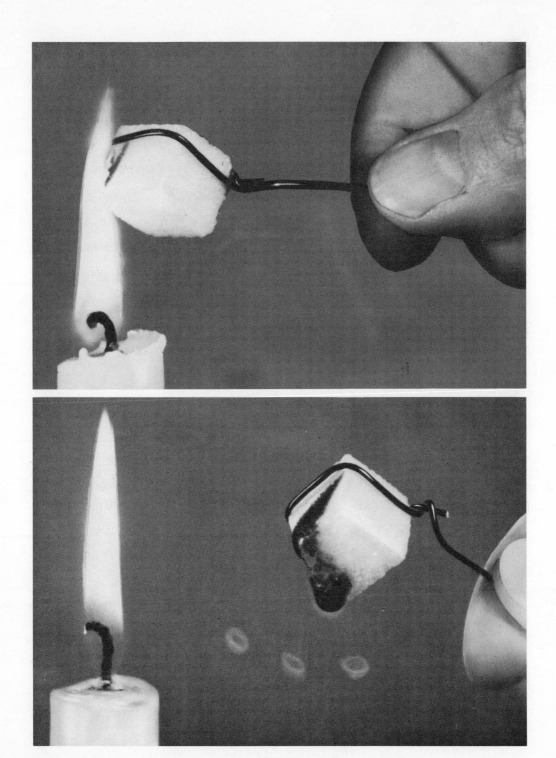

BLEACHING WITH OXYGEN

When we speak of anything combining with oxygen, we usually think of flame, heat and smoke. But _oxidation,_ as the chemist calls it, can also go on very quietly, and may even take place under water.

Bleaching is an operation of this kind. A common household bleach is sold under the name of Clorox. It is used to whiten clothes in the laundry, and its action depends on the fact that it furnishes oxygen. This oxygen then combines with the dyes or impurities to form compounds that are without color. Some disinfectants act in the same way. They produce oxygen which can oxidize bacteria, in effect burning them up.

Stir a few drops of ordinary writing ink into half a glass of water, making a fairly dark blue mixture. Add two or three drops of Clorox and stir again. The liquid will rapidly lose its dark color, becoming almost colorless as the dye in the ink is oxidized.

Bleaching is an important step in making cotton goods because the natural cotton fiber is not perfectly white. In the past, most bleaching of cloth was done by placing it in the sun. The rays of the sun can "fade out" colors by making the dye compounds break down, and oxidation is a similar process. Nowadays, the cloth manufacturer need not depend on the sun's shining; he bleaches his fabrics by the chemical method.

RUSTING OF IRON

The rusting of iron or steel is another example of slow oxidation.

Moisten a tuft of steel wool (like that used for cleaning pots and pans) and pack it into the bottom of a test tube. Stand the tube upside down in about half an inch of water in a glass. After a day or so you will notice that the water has gone up into the tube, just as in the experiment with the burning paper. The reason is the same—oxygen has combined with the iron in this case—but the change here has been much slower.

If you look closely at the metal you will see brown spots of rust—a compound of iron, oxygen and water.

In one of the most famous experiments in the history of chemistry, iron was allowed to rust and the rust was found to weigh slightly more than the original iron. This showed that something (oxygen) from the surrounding air was "captured" by the iron.

Rust is quite different from iron and steel. It is flaky and weak, while steel is tough and strong, so you can see that it is important to protect steel bridges and other structures from rusting. This is usually done by a covering of paint or by a plating of some other metal, so that the steel does not come in contact with the oxygen of the air. Even so, engineers tell us that several million dollars' worth of iron is wasted every year by rusting.

BURNING STEEL

In the last experiment iron was oxidized or "burned" at a slow rate. But iron can burn rapidly, too. Of course, a large piece of iron or steel will not be attacked by fire, but if you use thin strands of the metal the oxygen can get to it more easily and it will burn.

Take some strands of steel wool and twist them onto the end of a small stick that serves as a handle. Touch the tuft to a candle flame until the strands begin to sputter. Then pull it back from the flame and watch it burn. It will give off sparks and little drops of _iron oxide_ will fall off as the burning continues. You can see one of them in the picture.

IODINE AND STARCH

Stir a teaspoonful of flour into a small glass half full of very hot water. With a teaspoon let one or two drops of _tincture of iodine_ fall into the water. The entire liquid will turn dark blue.

This experiment is your introduction to two useful chemicals—_iodine_ and _starch_. Iodine is an element having the form of purple crystals, and tincture of iodine is a solution of these crystals in alcohol.

Starch is a compound of carbon, oxygen and hydrogen, and is found in plants. The blue color you noticed in the experiment was caused by starch from the flour acting on the iodine. Chemists use this color as a test to tell if starch is present in a material. See what happens when you put a drop of iodine on a bit of mashed potato or on a small piece of moistened white bread.

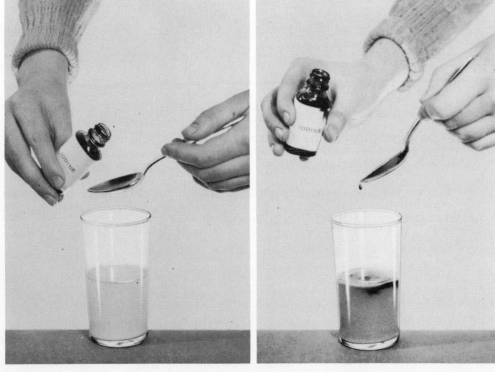

STARCH FROM POTATOES

The last test showed that potatoes contain starch. Here is a way of getting this starch out for further use in your home laboratory.

Peel and grate two large potatoes. Put this pulp into a handkerchief and squeeze it out into a small bowl about half full of water. Dip the handkerchief into the water several times, squeezing it out after each dipping. The water will become cloudy. Then let the water stand for a few minutes. A white powder will settle out. Carefully pour off most of the clearer water above and allow the rest to evaporate, leaving the dry powder. This is starch. Test a little of it with iodine, saving the remainder for the next experiment.

Starch is a material of many uses. As a food, it gives our bodies heat and energy. Corn, wheat, rye, rice and potatoes contain large amounts of this compound. When you eat such foods, chemicals that are present in the digestive juices change the starch to a kind of sugar that can be used directly by the body.

Starch is put onto cloth to give it weight and smoothness. The "glue" on envelopes and postage stamps is a starch product, and even some explosives are made from this compound.

CLOUDY LIQUIDS

In a previous experiment we saw how sugar can dissolve in water to form a clear mixture, or _solution._ If starch is mixed with water, it too seems to dissolve, but it does not form a true solution. Instead of breaking up into separate molecules in the water, as sugar did, the starch breaks into grains made up of thousands of molecules. These grains are not big enough to settle out, but form a _suspension_ in the water.

One of the best ways to tell the difference between a solution and a suspension is shown in the following test:

Put a teaspoonful of the potato starch from the last experiment into half a glass of water in a small pan. Heat over a low flame while stirring with a spoon. When the starch is boiled, as it is here or when used in the laundry, the tiny grains break open and form a jelly-like paste.

Now stir a few drops of this paste into a fresh glass of water. The starch seems to dissolve but a simple test shows that it does not really do this. Cut a small hole in a cardboard and hold it between a strong lamp and the glass of starch water. You will see the beam of light where it goes through the liquid because the starch particles _scatter_ the light. This does not happen with a true solution—try sugar water and see the difference in appearance.

Materials which form suspensions that do not settle out are called _colloids,_ and are very important in science and in industry. Your blood is a colloid; so is ice cream. Colloids play a large part in the making of glue, paint, cement, rubber and many other useful products.

FLAME TESTS

Chemists are often called upon to analyze materials—that is, to find out what they contain. A reliable way of testing to find certain elements is to note the color that the material produces when put in a flame.

Try this experiment: Turn on one burner of the kitchen range. Moisten the clean end of a used wooden match stick and dip it into a little salt, so that the crystals cling to it. Hold the end with the salt on it in the flame and notice the bright yellow color that appears. This yellow, which is deeper than that of a candle flame, tells the chemist that the element _sodium_ is present in the sample being tested. (Table salt is merely a compound of two elements, sodium and chlorine.) The flame test for sodium is so sensitive that a single crystal of salt would be enough to give color to about a million gas flames.

Using a fresh match, put some cream of tartar (which is used in baking) into the gas flame. Tiny reddish sparks stream off the match, as in the picture. This red color identifies the element _potassium_.

For still another test, get some boric acid from the medicine cabinet. The green color given to the flame tells us that an element called _boron_ is part of the compound known as boric acid.

Besides using flame tests like the ones you have just tried, chemists often make use of an instrument called a _spectroscope_ (see lower picture). Here, too, the material is heated, and the glow it gives off is broken up into its separate colors by the instrument. The resulting color pattern tells what elements make up the sample.

34

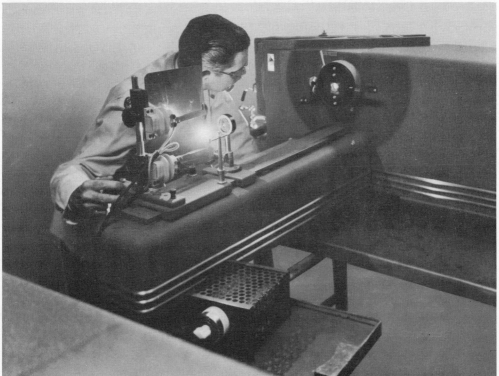

MAKING CARBON DIOXIDE

In some chemical actions, such as the explosion of gunpowder or dynamite, great quantities of gas are suddenly set free. The pressure of the gas produces the noise and damage which result. But where was all this gas before the powder was set off? It was "locked up" chemically in the solid material of the powder.

Let us set off a very mild and harmless form of explosion to show what happens: Get a large bottle with a well-fitting cork. Put about two tablespoons of baking soda into the bottle, using a folded piece of paper as described on page 8. Pour about two tablespoonfuls of vinegar into a test tube or small glass. Moisten the cork with water and hold it in one hand, the glass of vinegar in the other. Next, pour the vinegar into the jar and quickly insert the cork, but not too tightly. There will be a great fizzing and bubbling, and after a moment the cork will blow into the air with a loud pop!

And now let us see what went on. Baking soda is the common name for a chemical compound called _sodium_ _bicarbonate_. It consists of the elements sodium, hydrogen, carbon and oxygen. Vinegar contains a mild acid called _acetic_ _acid_. When the two are mixed, a chemical action takes place which sets free a gas called _carbon_ _dioxide_. The pressure of this gas builds up inside the bottle and finally blows the cork out.

When an explosive is set off the effects are similar, but much more sudden and destructive.

36

THE SODA WATER GAS

Here is another experiment with carbon dioxide:

Pour a tablespoonful of vinegar into a glass of water and add a table-spoonful of baking soda. Then drop three moth balls into the glass. Soon you will see many tiny bubbles of carbon dioxide forming on the moth balls.

The clinging bubbles act like little life preservers and make the moth balls rise to the top. Usually some of these bubbles break off when the surface is reached, and the ball then sinks because it is slightly denser than water. When enough bubbles have had time to gather, the story repeats. This may continue for a few hours before the chemicals are used up. Notice that some bubbles appear in all parts of the liquid, but more of them are formed on the rough surface of the moth balls.

The rising bubbles make the liquid look like soda water (soda water is simply plain water containing carbon dioxide that was forced into it when it was bottled).

The name "soda" water comes from the fact that the carbon dioxide was formerly made by the action of an acid on soda—just as in your experiment.

Another variety of carbon dioxide which you may know about is "dry ice." It is a solid, produced by cooling the gas until it forms crystals.

THE GAS THAT CHOKES FIRE

If a lighted kitchen match is held just inside the mouth of a milk bottle, it will continue to burn because it can get plenty of oxygen from the air. Try it.

Next fill the bottle with carbon dioxide by putting in a tablespoonful of baking soda and adding about a quarter of a cup of vinegar. As the carbon dioxide is set free, it gradually fills the bottle, at the same time pushing the air out. By the time foaming stops, the bottle is filled with this heavy gas, which stays in the bottle, just as water would.

Now repeat the test with the lighted match. This time the match will go out as soon as it is held in the neck of the bottle, as shown in the lower picture. The reason is that the match is surrounded by carbon dioxide and can get no air for burning.

This trial shows that nothing can burn in carbon dioxide. It also tells us that this gas is heavier than air, for the bottle remained filled with it in spite of the fact that there was no protecting cover.

This behavior of carbon dioxide makes it an ideal fire fighter. Many of the fire extinguishers you see in schools, factories and public buildings make use of this gas. When set into operation, a stream of gas is shot onto the fire, mixed with a soapy liquid which forms a foam so that the gas remains where it is directed.

Not only is it impossible for things to burn in carbon dioxide, but it is also impossible for animals to breathe in its presence. Animals need air to carry oxygen to the lungs. If they have only carbon dioxide instead of air to breathe, they get no oxygen and so cannot live.

40

CHANGING SUGAR INTO ALCOHOL

As you found out on page 22, sugar is a chemical compound of three elements: carbon, oxygen and hydrogen. The same three elements compose _alcohol_ but in different proportion, and it is possible to change sugar into alcohol very easily. The process is called _fermentation_.

Wine makers have been carrying on this operation for centuries, long before the chemistry of it was understood. Here's how to make an experiment:

Dissolve a teaspoonful of sugar in about one fourth glass of lukewarm water. Get a cake of yeast and crumple it into the water. Within a half hour you will see a spongy mass of bubbles form as in the picture. The alcohol is in the liquid below. The bubbles consist of carbon dioxide, which is set free when sugar is changed into alcohol.

You may not realize it, but yeast really consists of very simple living plants, something like the furry mold that forms on stale bread. The yeast plants produce a chemical which acts on the sugar molecules and makes them break up.

The purpose of using yeast in baking is to produce bubbles of carbon dioxide which raise the bread or cake batter and make it light.

FIRE PRODUCES WATER

With your mouth wide open, breathe on the blade of an ordinary dinner knife. Notice the film of mist that forms on the blade. Of course you see at once that this is merely some of the water vapor in your breath which _condensed_ when it touched the cooler metal.

Now to the real experiment. Run cold water over the knife to chill the blade, then wipe it dry. Hold the blade for a moment about three inches above a candle flame. On the lower side of the knife you will see the same film of moisture as before.

This result means that water came from the flame in some way. Let us see how this is possible. In the first place, the heat of the flame melts some wax, and this liquid wax rises in the wick. When it reaches the top of the wick it burns. Candle wax consists of compounds of carbon and hydrogen, as do most machine oils and gasoline. When any one of these burns, the hydrogen combines with oxygen in the air and the result is nothing more nor less than water.

Water formed by the burning of gasoline in a car passes out through the exhaust pipe. Every gallon of gasoline burned in the engine produces over three-quarters of a gallon of water.

In the burning of a candle, the carbon that is present in the wax is set free in the form of millions of tiny black particles. Heated by the flame, they give off the familiar yellow light that you see. In the case of an automobile engine, most of the carbon burns up to form _carbon dioxide_ (page 36) and _carbon monoxide,_ which is very deadly even when you breathe a tiny amount. The fact that there is carbon monoxide in the exhaust gas of a car is the reason the engine should never be run in a closed garage.

44

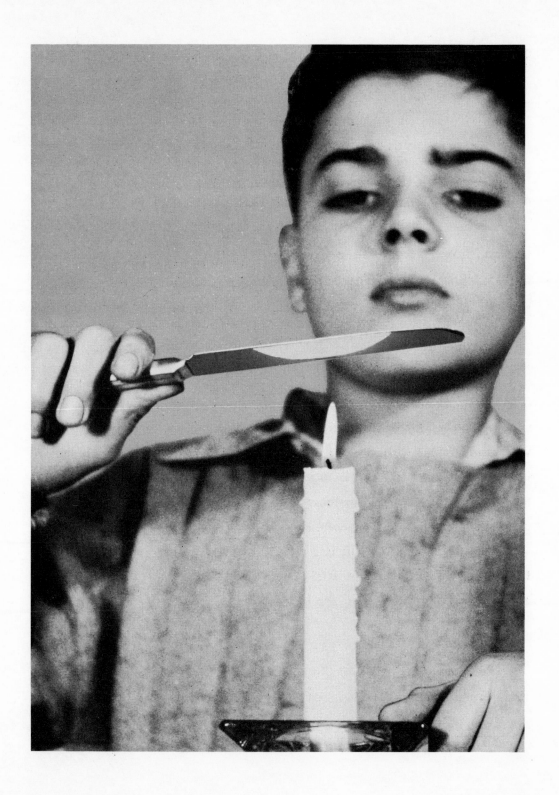

BREATHING PLANTS

If you were to ask a chemist what he considered the most important chemical process in the world he would not hesitate to answer, "The making of starch and sugar by plants."

A green plant is Nature's chemical laboratory. It is able to take carbon dioxide from the air and water from the soil and build them into starch and sugar. The process is made possible by the action of sunlight on the green coloring material of the plant. Chemists have not yet found a way to do this artificially.

If you have a growing plant in your home, preferably ivy or some vine-like plant, try this experiment: Fill a test tube to the very top with water and, using your thumb as a stopper, turn the tube upside down in a bowl of water. Now, being very careful to keep the mouth of the tube under water, take your thumb away and push a branch of the plant up inside the tube. Set the whole arrangement in the sun.

In a few hours you will find what seems to be a vacant space at the top of the tube. This space is really filled with oxygen which was produced by sunlight acting on the leaves of the plant.

Remember, as you do the experiment, that without this process there could be no life on earth because—directly or indirectly—we need plants for food.

CHEMICAL OPPOSITES

Sooner or later in working with chemistry we meet _acids_ and _bases_, the two great chemical opposites. You can be fairly sure that anything having a _sour_ taste contains an acid. Sour milk, for example, contains lactic acid, lemons contain citric acid and vinegar is impure acetic acid.

Bases have a _bitter_ taste. _Ammonia,_ which is a base, is water containing a compound called _ammonium hydroxide._ Sodium bicarbonate (baking soda) also has the effect of a base.

Being opposites, acids and bases can _neutralize_ each other when mixed, but just the right amount of each must be used. How can we tell when we have added the correct quantity of a base to "kill off" a certain amount of an acid? That is where we make use of a remarkable chemical called an _indicator_. It tells us, by changing color, whether the mixture has more base or more acid in it. Red cabbage contains a coloring matter which acts in this way.

Put a glassful of water in a pan, add half a glass of shredded red cabbage and bring it to a boil. Turn down the flame and let the mixture simmer for fifteen minutes. Pour the colored water into a glass and let it cool. Then put some of the liquid into a saucer, add one-quarter teaspoonful of baking soda and stir. The color will change from wine-red to a deep green. This means that the baking soda made the mixture _basic_. Now add vinegar little by little, stirring the liquid. At a certain point the color will turn to red again, showing that the mixture is now _acid_.

The indicator shows exactly when the right amount of acid has been added to neutralize the base. Indicators are very useful in controlling chemical processes in manufacturing.

METAL FROM THE OCEAN

Dissolve a level teaspoonful of Epsom salts crystals in one-quarter of a glass of water, stirring with a glass sipper or a stick. Notice that the liquid is perfectly clear. Now add about half an inch of ammonia and stir again. At once the liquid becomes cloudy. Let the glass stand for about five minutes and look at it again, and you will find that a jelly-like white mass has formed. This is a base called *magnesium hydroxide* which settles to the bottom of the glass after a few minutes.

In order to make this compound disappear we can neutralize it by adding about half an inch of vinegar and stirring. If some of the magnesium hydroxide is still left, add more vinegar until the liquid clears completely, as in the lower picture.

The water of the ocean has compounds of several valuable metals dissolved in it. Among the most useful is magnesium, and every gallon of sea water contains about one-seventh of an ounce of this metal. Recently it has been found possible to make these magnesium compounds settle out by changing them to magnesium hydroxide, just as in your experiment. After further chemical procedures, the magnesium is finally obtained in the form of a white metal that is lighter than even aluminum and so is very useful in making airplane parts.

USEFUL ARTICLES MADE OF SOUR MILK

When you look at a bottle of milk on the kitchen table you get no hint of the fact that the chemist can make such things as paint, glue, artificial wool and an ivory-like material from this healthful liquid. Yet millions of gallons of milk are used every year for such purposes. The wonder material in milk which makes this possible is called _casein_. Here is how you can prepare it:

Pour a pint of milk into an enameled pan and heat very gently until lukewarm. Remove from the flame and stirring constantly, pour in half a cup of vinegar. The milk will curdle at once. Continue to stir until the white curd gathers together in the form of a rubbery mass. Lift it out, remove the water by squeezing it like a sponge, and you have casein— the starting point for many chemical products.

When the chemist wishes to make articles of casein like those mentioned above, he first removes the casein from milk just as you did in your experiment. Then he dries this curd, grinds it to a powder, adds coloring matter and water, and kneads it into a dough. The mixture is pressed in a heated mold to give it the shape of the desired article and is hardened by dipping it into a chemical solution.

Many varieties of these so-called _plastics_ are known. Some of them are transparent. The bombardier compartment of the B-18 training ship shown on the opposite page is a good example of this type of plastic.

52

HOW SOAP ACTS

Put about one inch of water in a test tube. Add an equal amount of cooking oil (mineral oil or any other oil will do). Close the end of the tube with your thumb and shake the contents well. Notice that the oil breaks up into drops, but most of these drops come together again after about half a minute. This is probably what you expected, for you know that "oil and water don't mix." Also, note that the oil gathers at the top, the water at the bottom. The reason is that oil is less dense (or "lighter") than water.

Now repeat the experiment but instead of using plain water, dissolve half a teaspoonful of soap powder in half a cup of water. Pour about an inch of this soapy liquid into another test tube and add oil as before. This time, when you shake the tube the result is a milky white _emulsion_ which separates out only after a long time.

The chemical nature of soap enables it to keep the small drops or globules of oil suspended in the water. This is really why soap has a cleaning action. Usually, dirt clings to your clothes and skin because a film of grease holds it there. The purpose of soap is to break up this film so that the dirt can be washed away.

Another very familiar example of an emulsion is milk, which consists of tiny drops of fat suspended in water. On standing, the drops of fat will gather at the top to some extent to form cream.

54

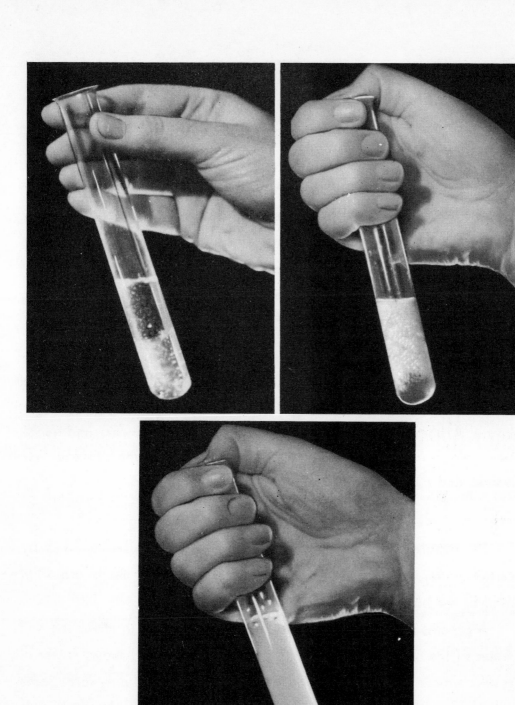

HARD WATER ROBS SOAP

In some parts of the country, the water has a great amount of mineral matter dissolved in it. We say this water is _hard._ Hard water makes washing very difficult because soap does not lather well in it. The reason is that the dissolved minerals in the water combine chemically with the soap and actually destroy it.

In order to see how this happens, try an experiment with water that is purposely made hard. Dissolve a teaspoonful of Epsom salts in about one-third of a glass of water. In another glass containing an equal amount of water dissolve some soap. Pour the contents of the first glass into the second. A white scum forms. Rub some between your fingers and notice how sticky it is. This is a compound containing the soap, which is now wasted and no longer free to perform its cleaning action.

The dissolved minerals that make water hard can be removed by certain _water softening_ chemicals. Washing soda and borax are often used in the home laundry for this purpose.

A process similar to water softening can be used to make the salt water of the ocean fit to drink. The lower photograph shows a test of a new way of doing this. Survivors adrift at sea need only force some salt water through the chemically-treated bags in order to obtain drinkable water to keep them alive.

HOW CHEMISTS USE ELECTRICITY

A battery produces an electric current by chemical action. It is also true that chemical changes can be brought about by electricity.

Tape together two flashlight cells so that the metal bottom of one makes good contact with the center terminal in the top of the other. Scrape a clean place on the side of the lower cell and twist the cleaned end of a piece of copper bell wire firmly around it. Wind the other end of the wire around a pencil to form a "pigtail." Fashion a similar pigtail on a second length of wire.

Now dissolve two teaspoonfuls of salt in a glass of water. Completely fill a test tube with the solution and pour the rest into a soup plate. Using your thumb as a stopper, turn the tube upside down in the liquid in the plate. (Remove your thumb while keeping the mouth of the tube under water.) Now, still keeping the open end of the tube under water, insert in it the pigtail from the wire attached to the lower flashlight cell. Lay the second pigtail in the salt water and touch the other end of this wire to the center terminal of the upper cell, as in the photograph. The salt water completes the circuit and you will see many fine bubbles streaming off the pigtail. These are bubbles of _hydrogen_ gas which collects at the top of the tube. The hydrogen was set free from the water by the electric current.

At the other wire, a gas called _chlorine_ is produced from the salt. It does not bubble off but combines with the copper of the wire, tarnishing it. After the current has been on for a little while, you will notice that the salt water has turned slightly blue. This color is caused by the copper which combines with the chlorine.

In large chemical plants, chlorine is made electrically in just this way.

58

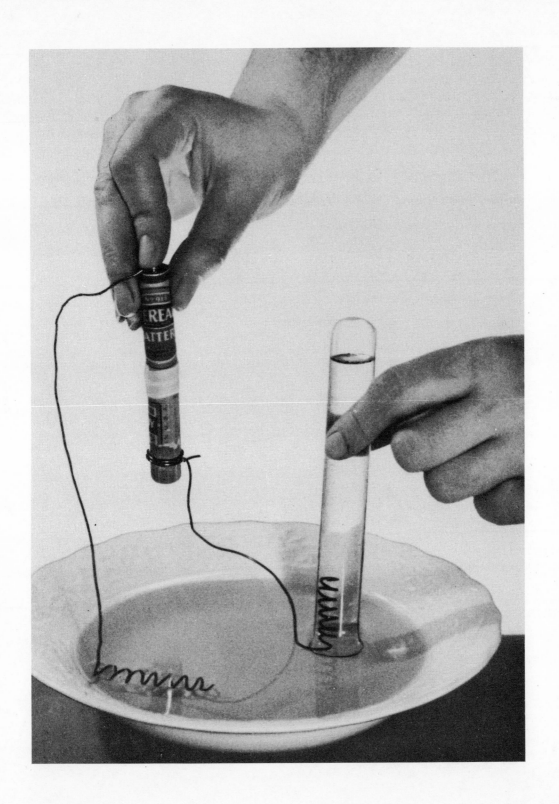